MW00593149

Lady
GAGA

SARAH PARVIS

Andrews McMeel
Publishing, LLC

Kansas City • Sydney • London

Produced by

DOWNTOWN
BOOKWORKS INC.

President · Julie Merberg

Senior Vice President · Patty Brown

Designer · Brian Michael Thomas/
Our Hero Productions

Special Thanks · Pam Abrams, Caroline Bronston,
Michael Galante, Emily Simon

10 11 12 13 14 TEP 10 9 8 7 6 5 4 3 2 1

ISBN-13: 978-0-7407-9795-8
ISBN-10: 0-7407-9795-6
Library of Congress Control Number: 2010924911

www.andrewsmcmeel.com

TABLE OF CONTENTS

Meet Stefani G.

*L*ong before the lacy masks, disco balls, and otherworldly outfits, Lady Gaga was simply Stefani Germanotta. Born Stefani Joanne Angelina Germanotta on March 28, 1986, to Italian-American parents (Joseph and Cynthia), the future starlet grew up on the Upper West Side of Manhattan.

POP QUIZ

Where was Lady Gaga born?

Her love of performing began at an early age. "I was always an entertainer. I was a ham as a little girl and I am a ham now," she shared on her official Web site. When she was little, she would pop her favorite old-school tapes into her tiny plastic cassette player, and sing along with '80s pop stars such as Cyndi Lauper and Michael Jackson. But her musical tendencies weren't limited to a little lip-synching or imitating tunes on

the radio. At four years old, she learned to play songs on the piano by ear. By thirteen, she was writing piano music.

Hard as it may be for her fans to imagine now, but back in the day, Stefani attended the all-girl Convent of the Sacred Heart. Located on a picturesque corner of the Upper East Side, Sacred Heart is an exclusive and academically challenging institution. Like the other girls at school, she wore

"I didn't fit in in high school, and I felt like a freak. So I like to create this atmosphere for my fans where they feel like they have a freak in me to hang out with, and they don't feel alone."

a modest kilt and followed the nuns' rules. She studied classical piano and performed in school plays. Looking back on her teen years, Lady Gaga acknowledges that she was mostly a studious good girl, though she admits to feeling stifled at times. On days when she was allowed to break free from her uniform, she said, "I used to

POP QUIZ

A pair of famous sisters also attended the Convent of the Sacred Heart. Name these heiresses.

A: Paris and Nicky Hilton

really get made fun of for being either too provocative, or too eccentric, so I started to kind of tone it down."

After high school, she attended the Tisch School of the Arts, part of New York University. Though she'd felt insecure in high school, Lady Gaga did not hold back in college. She wore crazy clothes and pursued her love of music. Eventually, she dropped out of Tisch to live the life of a starving artist. "I got three jobs waitressing," she said.

did you know?

Lady Gaga designed and built her own costumes when she was an up-and-comer in New York's burlesque scene.

"I was good at serving Italian food in heels." Away from school and her family, she hung out with other young creative people and began performing at dive bars, burlesque venues, and any clubs that would allow her onstage. On these small stages, she learned to make the toughest crowds take notice.

"The rumors I am a dab hand in the kitchen are completely true. I come from an Italian family—what more can I say? I love to cook. I am really good at Italian food. So I make great meatballs, pasta, and all sorts. I love it. When I get the chance, I make a mean meal."

She worked her way through the club scene and, in 2005, Def Jam Recordings decided to take a chance on her. Sadly, Stefani's first recording contract was short-lived. She was hurt when Def Jam dropped her with barely any explanation, but did not let it hold her back. Little did she know at the time, but success was just around the corner for Lady Gaga. She only needed a push in the right direction. And that push came in the form of singer-songwriter, producer extraordinaire Akon.

did you know?

Lady Gaga was still known as Stefani Germanotta when she signed with Def Jam in 2005.

Back in 2007, Lady Gaga performed at Lollapalooza in Chicago. Though she was relatively unknown on the national level, she shared the stage with long-standing musical acts such as Pearl Jam, Daft Punk, Muse, Snow Patrol, and the Roots. The then-unknown brunette was no headliner. Instead, she played during the daytime in a disco-ball bikini.

WHAT'S IN A NAME?

The future pop diva went from Stefani to stage name in a matter of minutes. And the inspiration came in the form of a mistyped text message from a friend. In 2006, the aspiring songstress was working with music producer Rob Fusari in his New Jersey studio. Rob likened Stefani's vocal style to that of Freddie Mercury, the late great singer of the band Queen. When she arrived in the studio to meet him, Rob would often sing the lyrics to Queen's "Radio Ga Ga" as a sort of hello. One day, he sent her a text message that was supposed to simply say "Radio Ga Ga." Somehow, a typo and/or a glitch in his phone's autocorrect program changed "Radio" to "Lady," and Stefani's star persona was born.

Music and Inspiration

*W*hen Akon stumbled across Lady Gaga in 2007, he knew he had unearthed a special talent. "At the end of the day," he said a year after he'd signed her to his KonLive label (part of Interscope Records), "she's one of those rare finds. A diamond in the rough that you just have to polish out and let shine, and that's exactly what she's doing."

She worked a little as a songwriter for Interscope, penning lyrics for artists such as Britney Spears, New Kids on the Block, and the Pussycat Dolls. But the release of her debut single, "Just Dance," made it clear that Lady Gaga needed to be onstage. The single, which also featured Colby O'Donis, was a huge hit on the club scene. Little by little, it broke into radio. By the time "Poker

did you know?

Lady Gaga is only the third musician (and first American singer) with three Billboard No. 1 hits on a debut album. The other two are Avril Lavigne and Ace of Base.

Face" hit the airwaves, pop fans had already taken notice. "Poker Face" was an immediate chart topper.

Lady Gaga's first full-length album, *The Fame*, featured a trio of No. 1 hits. After "Just Dance" and "Poker Face" came "LoveGame." About her first album, she explained, "*The Fame* is

"I'm obsessed with 1950s science fiction monster movies. The inspiration for the album comes from the sort of dark infatuation with monsters and apocalypse and darkness and theater. So you will see in [*The Fame Monster*] a more scary Lady Gaga, if I wasn't already freaking you out enough."

about how anyone can feel famous." She really wanted the album and her style of music to inspire and be part of a pop art movement. In Lady Gaga's opinion, "What has been lost in pop music these days is the combination of the visual and the imagery of the artist, along with the music—and both are just as

important." To recapture the glory days of glam rockers and their superfans, she has drawn on the inspiration of such artists as Madonna, David Bowie, Queen, Grace Jones, the New York Dolls, and Black Sabbath.

Though Lady Gaga clearly knows how to put on a memorable show, she isn't all glitter gloves and mirror masks. She's also got the musical chops to keep fans' ears yearning for more.

"I always loved rock and pop and theater. When I discovered Queen and David Bowie is when it really came together for me and I realized I could do all three."

LADY GAGA
on art

"I went to art school. I studied pop culture. I know everything about music and iconography: pop, cultural, and religious. I'm self-manufactured."

"I'm here to make great music and inspire people."

"Right now, the only thing that I am concerned with in my life is being an artist. I had to suppress it for so many years in high school because I was made fun of, but now I'm completely insulated in my box of insanity and I can do whatever I like."

"I eat, sleep, breathe, and bleed every inch of my work. I'd absolutely die if I couldn't be an artist."

HAUS OF GAGA

Lady Gaga may be a force to be reckoned with, but she isn't the only creative mind behind her wild costumes and stage sets. To create her aesthetic, she has assembled a group of stylists, artists, and creative folks she trusts. Inspired by Andy Warhol's Factory in the 1960s, this design team is known as the Haus of Gaga. She credits this group of friends and colleagues with helping her continue to create fresh, thought-provoking pop music. "They are my heart and soul," she has said of the Haus of Gaga. "They believe in me, and they look at me like a mother and daughter and sister, with pride and love."

LITERARY INSPIRATION

Lady Gaga has said many times that she consults her favorite book every day. And what is this special tome? Rainer Maria Rilke's *Letters to a Young Poet*. She even has a quote from the poet tattooed in German on her arm! It says:

In the deepest hour of the night, confess to yourself that you would die if you were forbidden to write. And look deep into your heart where it spreads its roots, the answer, and ask yourself, must I write?

Fashion Forward

*L*ady Gaga has made a name for herself as much for her talent as for her shocking sense of style. She doesn't shy away from the wackiest costumes and accessories. As she put it, "When I'm writing music, I'm thinking about the clothes I want to wear onstage. It's all about everything all together—performance art, pop performance art, fashion." If it grabs attention, she'll wear it. With gusto. Who but Lady Gaga would wear a red plastic dress and glittery red eye sequins to meet the Queen of England?

One of the special things about her wardrobe is that she refuses to limit herself to fabrics. She's been known to cover herself in the most creative materials. Whether made of bubbles, mirror balls, or countless stuffed Kermit the Frogs, her outfits are one of a kind and sure to cause a stir. During the 52nd annual Grammy Awards, she made her entrance in one gown, wore another costume onstage, and yet another while seated in the audience. Her first outfit of the evening included a bright yellow

POP QUIZ

Who designed Lady Gaga's out-of-this-world red carpet dress for the 2010 Grammy Awards?

A: Armani Privé

wig and a pale-pink dress enveloped by shimmery hoops that made her look like a one-woman solar system. Instead of a boring old clutch, she carried a silver star-shaped sparkle accessory. For her audience outfit, she took her headwear to bold, new heights. She sported a glittering geometric headdress, sparkling body-suit, winged jacket, and extra-tall jewel-encrusted platform shoes.

Lady Gaga doesn't confine her creativity to her clothing. She has also been known to decorate her body. At the amfAR gala in February 2010, she actually glued hundreds of pearls to her face, legs, and body to create a look that redefined the phrase "showing off your pearly whites." Hot-pink lipstick was the only color she wore that night.

Just as she strives to push boundaries musically by melding

did you know?

The pink lipstick that Lady Gaga wore to the amfAR gala is actually named for her. Created by MAC, the special-edition makeup was sold to help raise funds for AIDS research.

commercial pop with more interesting and thought-provoking themes and lyrics, she likes to push boundaries with her fashion. Her name lands in the press both for what she wears and what she doesn't (for example, pants). Whether she's sporting a somewhat see-through lace onesie or a skirt that doesn't actually cover her backside, she has made it clear that she is not afraid to show off her body in the pursuit of fame. Lady Gaga doesn't try to be polished or pretty either. She's not afraid to appear onstage in a knotted wig, or covered in dirt or stage blood. She'll sneer and snarl and fight her way through a song, giving the audience as much performance art as pop song.

Lady Gaga and her team of stylists don't limit themselves to her costumes and accessories. Her pianos get the royal treatment, too. At the February 2010 Brit Awards in London, both she and her instrument were draped in billowing white tulle. She dedicated that evening's performance, a slow version of the song "Telephone," to fashion designer Alexander McQueen, who had recently committed suicide.

One of Lady Gaga's most remarkable outfits was her infamous bubble dress. She explained, "The bubble installation was inspired by a dress Hussein Chalayan made a few years ago. I couldn't get the dress, because it's, like, half-a-million dollars in a museum somewhere, but I remade it and I built a piano somewhat inspired by it."

LADY GAGA
on fashion

"I'm an outspoken and extreme dresser. I am inspired by photography and art, but mostly by New York."

"I'm just trying to change the world one sequin at a time."

"I'd love to have my own collection. It's something I want to accomplish. I find Donatella a fashion icon and, in many ways, fashion and music go together."

"I'm part designer lover, part fashionista, and part handmade garments on my own. I made a lot of my clothes. . . . the hair bow is cheap to make. You can make it yourself."

High-Octane Performances

*O*n the story *Peter Pan*, the tiny fairy Tinker Bell drinks poison and Peter explains that if people clap really hard to prove they still believe in fairies, she might live. "I'm kind of like Tinker Bell," Lady Gaga told an audience in Boston at the start of her Monster Ball tour. "See, if you don't clap for Tinker Bell, she dies!"

Lady Gaga has shared her philosophy on performing: "I live right here in the moment. I live onstage. I don't own a house. I don't spend money on those things. I live out of a suitcase and I make music and art and I spend every dollar that I make onstage."

Some incredible things have come from her dedication to her audience. During the 2009 American Music Awards, she sported a flesh-colored unitard and an alien-looking headdress while she and her crew of backup dancers performed a spirited version

did you know?

Lady Gaga suffers from stage fright.

of "Bad Romance." Then, she used her guitar stand to shatter one side of a glass cube. After climbing inside, she played "Speechless" on a burning piano. To the screams of her fans, she shattered bottle after bottle on the piano keys. During an elaborate number at the MTV Video Music Awards, she acted out her own bloody murder. She has played a raised piano while sitting in a chair hoisted 30 feet above the ground by chains. She has set off explosives on her own bodice and sung songs from giant bathtubs—all to keep audiences challenged and entertained. And it is working. Fans find her brand of performance-art-meets-pop both exciting and intriguing.

Lady Gaga admits to being a total perfectionist when it comes to her elaborate shows. "I'm very bossy," she has shared. "I can scream my head off if I see one light fixture out. I'm very detailed—every minute of the show has got to be perfect." Simply put, she wants to blow her audience's mind with each and every performance.

Gaga's wild performances are not confined to the stage. Her videos

"Being provocative is not just about getting people's attention. It's about saying something that really affects people in a real way, in a positive way."

are often mini-movies, with constant costume changes, backup dancers, and plenty of provocative visuals. In the award-winning "Paparazzi" video, Lady Gaga is a celebrity nearly killed by a fame-hungry boyfriend. She makes a comeback and takes her revenge. About the song, Lady Gaga has explained, "On one level it is about wooing the paparazzi and wanting fame. . . . But, it's also about wanting a guy to love you and the struggle of whether you can have success or love or both."

> "My message as a woman, to my fans, is always: Love yourself, free yourself, be whoever you want to be."

She is particularly fond of the video for "Bad Romance," which features some major dance moves in a gritty underground-club setting. But, after filming the "Telephone" video with Beyoncé, she said, "I feel so bad for the 'Bad Romance' video 'cause the 'Telephone' video's so much better." Lady Gaga told an interviewer that she and Beyoncé had a great time working together. "We're so very different in our approaches, but somehow when we come together it's really magical." Her shocking stage shows and intense videos keep her fans on their toes . . . and music lovers just can't wait to see what she'll do next.

Decked out like grubby monsters, Lady Gaga and Elton John performed together during the 52nd annual Grammy Awards on January 31, 2010. She kicked off the number with a slow version of "Poker Face" before being dumped down a chute labeled "Rejected." Then Lady Gaga and the renowned British crooner took their places at a two-sided piano decorated with severed arms. Together, they performed a mash-up of "Speechless" and Elton's hit "Your Song." Many thought it was one of the most memorable Grammy performances ever.

At the MOCA 30th-anniversary gala in November 2009 in L.A., Lady Gaga played a rotating pink piano decorated with butterflies. The look for the instrument was designed by artist Damien Hirst, who is best known for provocative art pieces such as a dissected shark in formaldehyde and a diamond-encrusted skull.

GAGA GIVES BACK

Along with '80s pop icon Cyndi Lauper, Lady Gaga is one of the faces of MAC cosmetics' Viva Glam campaign, which aims to spread the word about safe sex and to support people living with HIV and AIDS. The two singing divas have designed their own lipstick colors (bubblegum pink for Gaga and fire-engine red for Cyndi). All proceeds from the lipsticks will go to the MAC AIDS Fund. She also threw her name into the moneymaking mix for the relief efforts after a devastating earthquake struck Haiti in January 2010. She created a special-edition Lady Gaga Haiti T-shirt. All proceeds from the T-shirt sales went to help those struggling with the aftermath of the quake. She also donated the proceeds from ticket and merchandise sales from one New York performance of her Monster Ball tour. In addition to her AIDS charity work and donations for Haiti, Lady Gaga is an outspoken advocate for gay rights.

MEDIA MONSTER

Lady Gaga knows a thing or two about how the media business works. If she says or does something wild, journalists and bloggers will write all about it. The more outrageous outfits she wears in a day, the more attention she gets. The taller the wig, the more dangerous the heels, the more shocking the getup, the more images appear online and in magazines for Gaga-watchers to ogle. And Lady Gaga seems to know that. Performance artist, fashionista, fashion disaster, or trendsetter? However people categorize Lady Gaga, there is no doubt that she has a lot more up her sleeve.

LADY GAGA'S awards

Grammy Awards
2010   **Best Dance Recording for "Poker Face"**
2010   **Best Dance/Electronic Album for**
       The Fame

People's Choice Awards
2010   **Favorite Pop Artist**
2010   **Favorite Breakout Artist**

The Brit Awards
2010   **International Album for *The Fame***
2010   **International Female Solo Artist**
2010   **International Breakthrough Act**

Teen Choice Awards
2009   **Choice Music Hook-up for "Just Dance"**
       with Colby O'Donis

MTV Video Music Awards
2009   **Best New Artist for "Poker Face"**
2009   **Best Special Effects for "Paparazzi"**
2009   **Best Art Direction for "Paparazzi"**

"If people think Gaga is over-the-top and decadent now, I'm afraid for them; they have no idea what's to come."